THE
THANK YOU
BOOK

THE THANK YOU BOOK

First published in the Republic of Ireland in 2010 by

The Irish Hospice Foundation

Morrison Chambers, 32 Nassau St, Dublin 2, Ireland

Edited by Róisín Ingle

Design by AMP Visual.com

Printed in the EU by Spectrum Print Co. Ltd

ISBN-13: 978-0-9566590-0-2

Go raibh míle maith agat
*I thank you a thousand times**

The Celtic tradition laid great emphasis on gratitude. Conversation was replete with *buíochas* (thanks) for everything, and gratitude was communicated in *beannachtaí* (blessings) and *seanfhocail* (proverbs) about everyday life. Gratitude was felt for the gift of life, for safe passage through it and 'happy' departure from it. The scope of gratitude was as wide as life itself and beyond.

The source of this gratitude lay in faith. Deep in the Celtic psyche there was a sense of divine presence, in which even at subconscious levels people felt held in the hand of God. *Buíochas le Dia* (thanks be to God) was attached to every sentence and continues to be echoed in conversation to the present day.

This tradition of gratitude is still with us. The richness of people's contributions to *The Thank You Book* confirms this. They show hearts replete with thankfulness. We are grateful when people spend time with us, ask how we are and stick by us without judgment. We absorb the right word said at a key moment, a gentle touch, a generous greeting, a broad smile, sympathetic eye-contact, shared humour and everyday courtesies, all of which influence how we feel about ourselves and the world we live in. We value friendship, listening and laughter; the support of family and the kindness of strangers. We are grateful for gratitude itself.

The psychological benefits of gratitude are enormous. The process of recognising, recounting, appreciating and articulating that for which we are grateful has been validated within the disciplines of psychology and psychotherapy. The transformative power of positive affirmation, the neuro-psychological benefits of 'mindfulness' and the healing potential of optimism have each been recognised.

It is good to be grateful, and the routine of writing about it increases our gratitude. The practice of gratitude enhances mental health, physical well-being and emotional stability. It dilutes stress; it gives courage and hope. It can help us set goals and achieve them. When we are sad, gratitude can remind us of the good things that have also come our way. And gratitude is like love: the more we express it, the more we experience it.

Developing a grateful disposition is important for children too. Gratitude reassures children of their worth, increases their sense of security, reduces envy, and encourages generosity and the development of altruism in later life. Knowing how to say 'thank you' is important because of the social significance of those words, and parents begin social training by reminding their children to say 'thank you' when kindness is shown.

Gratitude is an emotion that is felt, experienced and learned, and it can be developed further for psychotherapeutic benefit. This is how *The Thank You Book* unites two important psychological strategies: keeping a diary and developing gratitude. Narrative psychology affirms the benefits of writing our story. Positive psychology affirms the advantage of focusing on what is positive in that account. To tell our own story to ourselves within the safety of the page to which we alone have access; to select, organise and record what matters to us, has long been recognised as a powerful process and potent therapeutic tool. To do so with the emphasis on gratitude expands this exercise into second psychological effect.

And if there is someone we wish we had thanked, it is not too late to do so. What we cannot say in words we might say in deed, with the gift of *The Thank You Book*. Those who are past being told may not be past knowing, and in *The Thank You Book* we can write and release our gratitude to them. Writing unlocks these feelings with positive psychological result.

The Thank You Book allows us to heal the past by identifying that which was good; it influences with gratitude the life we live now, and it shapes the future with awareness of what we may become. May writing in it bring you a hundred thousand experiences of the warmth in which you are held by others and the good that surrounds you each day.

My own first entry in this book will be to record how grateful I am to be a contributor to it.

Míle buíochas.
Dr. Marie Murray, *Clinical Psychologist*
* *Literally: May you have a thousand kindnesses*

INTRODUCTION
or
Why this is not just another notebook

The Thank You Book is a place for all that is precious and meaningful and funny and uplifting and lovely in your life. I have science on my side when I tell you that this is not just another notebook. We should have put a warning sticker on the cover: "This notebook is good for your health".

Still, it doesn't come naturally to everyone, this gratitude business. Some people (maybe even you) will be sceptical about the benefits of sitting down to write a gratitude list in a notebook called *The Thank You Book*. To others, the suggestion will sound too corny, too self-helpy, too Oprah. And yet, according to experts in the art of gratitude, even if we are full of doubt and derision when we begin, thankfulness will find a way of wrapping itself around us, like a warm coat on a bitterly cold day. Even if we start off as sceptics, eventually gratitude will win us over, toppling our half-empty glass and opening our eyes to the beauty of how things really are.

Religions and philosophies through the ages have embraced gratitude as an authentic spiritual path, but it's only recently that the science of gratitude has been studied in any great detail. Robert Emmons, a US-based Professor of Psychology, is the co-author of a study called "*Counting Blessings versus Burdens*". As part of the study a group of people were asked to keep a daily diary of five things for which they were grateful. Emmons found that these people rated higher on the happiness index than another group who, for the same period of the experiment, were asked to record their daily hassles and irritants. The grateful group also slept better, exercised more, had less illness, increased energy and were more optimistic about their lives.

"When individuals start a daily gratitude journal, they begin to feel a greater sense of connectedness to the world. After a few weeks people who follow this routine feel better about themselves, have more energy and feel more alert," he says.

Gratitude can be a quiet kind of emotion,

passive and humble and unassuming. This notebook is a place where you can reflect on all those everyday blessings: you find the pair of glasses you thought you'd lost, or the train isn't late for once or you manage to find a parking space, or someone you've been missing gets in touch just to say hello.

Gratitude can also be powerful and overwhelming, stopping you in your tracks. So this notebook is a place to celebrate the profundity of your experiences. The joy of being alive in the world. The magic in a West of Ireland sunset. The privilege of being loved unconditionally by family or friends, loved for who you are, exactly as you are.

I've only been writing gratitude lists for a few months. At first I was self conscious and I struggled. I was writing my lists as though somebody was looking over my shoulder, telling me that this 'thank you' was too trivial, that one cheesier than a wheel of Brie. When I stopped worrying what other people might think if they discovered the contents of my notebook, I started to write from my heart.

I wrote lists that included those random life moments: freewheeling on my bike, wind in my hair, feeling that everything was just as it should be. I wrote about the girl I saw in town with the torn fishnets and pink hair, blessing herself as she walked past a church. I wrote about a perfect egg sandwich, a stolen hour of sleep, the smell of the Liffey at dawn. I wrote about the soft touch of my children's hands. I wrote about the people I love, who love me.

Whatever you decide to write in these pages will be perfect. Perhaps it will take you a while to get going. Perhaps you will be inspired by other peoples 'thank you' messages sprinkled throughout this book. I've found it helps to write when you have time to be still, when there are no distractions, when you have five minutes peace. Do it your way.

Most of all, write when it feels as though you have nothing to be grateful for. Because this is when gratitude sneaks up on a person, gently forcing them to notice things that have remained hidden up until then. One thing that becomes clear when you start to write daily gratitude lists is that there is always, always a reason to give thanks. As the Buddha said: "Let us rise up and be thankful, for if we didn't learn a lot today, at least we learned a little, and if we didn't learn a little, at least we didn't get sick, and if we got sick, at least we didn't die; so, let us all be thankful".

Thank you for buying this book. I wish you all the best with your gratitude practice.

Róisín Ingle, Dublin, August 2010

Photography by Yvette Monahan, studioseventyseven photography

Sculpture and Photography by Seamus Gill

'Gratitude is a
quality similar to electricity:
it must be produced and
discharged and
used up in order
to exist at all'

William Faulkner

Thank You

'I felt gratitude, therefore I believed.' I have always been deeply thankful for those words by the poet Czeslaw Milosz. There is universal grá in that gratitude, and even though 'believed' is without a grammatical object, it's still an act of faith and a defiance of nihilism.

Seamus Heaney

SEAMUS HEANEY

That day, when you stopped
& asked "How are you"...
It meant everything...

Thank you

Christy Moore [signature]

CHRISTY MOORE

Thank You

Thank you for being
So cheerful and
full of hope
For seeing huge lights
at the end of dark
tunnels and patches
of blue in overcast
Skies
For believing that
things will work
out well and that
there is happiness
ahead!

Maeve Binchy

MAEVE BINCHY

Those lines around my eyes
were caused by laughing,
not frowning, and for
that I thank you.

Fiona Looney

FIONA LOONEY

**Thank you for listening without judging.
you are a true friend.**
Bill Hughes

Thank you,
for all the
times you were there
to laugh with me when
times were good. For
supporting me when things
were difficult. It's said
that if you have a
friend you have a fortune.
I'm rich because of your
friendship.

Daniel O'Donnell

DANIEL O'DONNELL

"Thank - You"

Thank You to the great
WRITERS who gave me the
'wine of astonishment' and to
the great wine-growers,
who gave me the wine.

Edna O'Brien

EDNA O'BRIEN

THANK YOU,
FOR ALL THE
TIMES YOU
HAVE FORGIVEN
ME.

JOHN KELLY

THANK YOU

You kept me safe
with your arms around me
when the rest of the world
was gone away.
I'd have been lost
without you.

PAT INGOLDSBY

55

Thank you.

You said ' You are strong. You can do
this. Listen to your heart. You know,
you were right, and it changed my life.
For always being on my side, no
matter what, I thank you.

SARAH WEBB

Thank you to St. Francis Hospice,
Raheny,
For Renewing my faith
in human Kindness x

BRENDAN GLEESON

For

Breath

Gabriel
Byrne

New York
April '10

GABRIEL BYRNE

Thank you.

For all the little unremembered acts of kindness & of love which I have experienced from you through my life, I just want to say

Thank you.

Gay Byrne

GAY BYRNE

Thank you.
Too late for you to hear it now, in your grave. Thank you for the foundation, and then for letting me loose.

Timothy O'Grady

TIMOTHY O'GRADY

Thank you for
encouraging me to leave
the safe harbour.
You are my joy.

Shane Hogan

SHANE HOGAN

Thank you
For allowing me to be sad,
to be quiet,
to relax.
Most people only want to see the bright me
You can manage all shades.

Maria Doyle Kennedy

MARIA DOYLE KENNEDY

Thank you.

I simply want to say
thank you for making
it better.

Maeve Friel

MAEVE FRIEL

He was a man who hated any physical show of affection. We had been through a long journey together, and the debt was *all* on my side. One day he got up rather awkwardly and crossed the room to me, and embraced me. "Thank you", he said."

SEBASTIAN BARRY

Thank you, for being You, and for allowing me to be me.

Cecelia Ahern

CECELIA AHERN

Gratitude
is the sign
of noble
souls.

Aesop
(620—560 BC)

"If the only prayer you said in
your whole life was, "thank
you," that would suffice"

Meister Eckhart

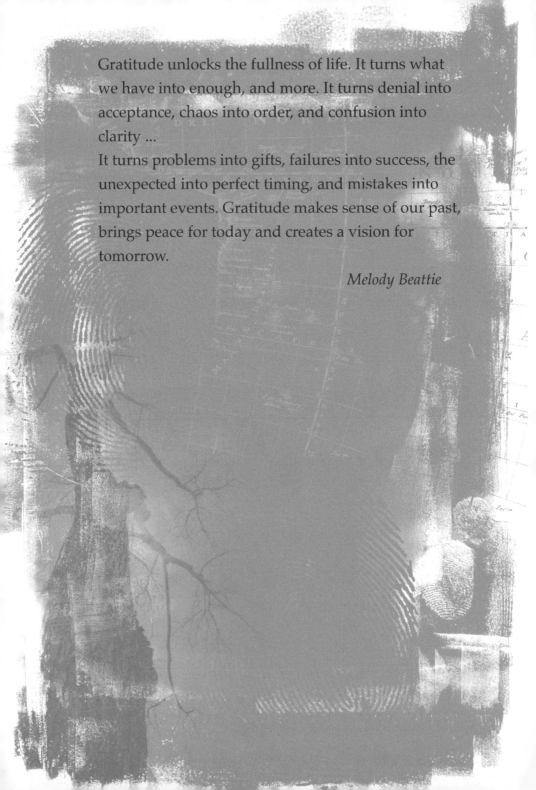

Gratitude unlocks the fullness of life. It turns what we have into enough, and more. It turns denial into acceptance, chaos into order, and confusion into clarity ...

It turns problems into gifts, failures into success, the unexpected into perfect timing, and mistakes into important events. Gratitude makes sense of our past, brings peace for today and creates a vision for tomorrow.

Melody Beattie

Gratitude is something of which none of us can give too much. For on the smiles, the thanks we give, our little gestures of appreciation, our neighbours build their philosophy of life.

A. J. Cronin

"Saying thank you is more
than good manners.
It is good spirituality"
Alfred Painter

EVERY TIME WE REMEMBER TO SAY "THANK YOU" WE EXPERIENCE NOTHING LESS THAN HEAVEN ON EARTH.

SARAH BAN BREATHNACH

WHERE THERE IS GRATITUDE,
THERE IS
HUMILITY,
AS OPPOSED
TO PRIDE

RACHEL WOODS

THANK YOU FOR
KNOWING ME INSIDE
OUT AND LOVING
ME ANYWAY —
RÓISÍN INGLE

Thank You,

I knew right away that I had not met your like before, your light shining and you so clearly free of a single judgement gene. The good life began through your non-judgemental regard and you remain the paramount influence in my life. And don't we laugh!!!

Lee Dunne

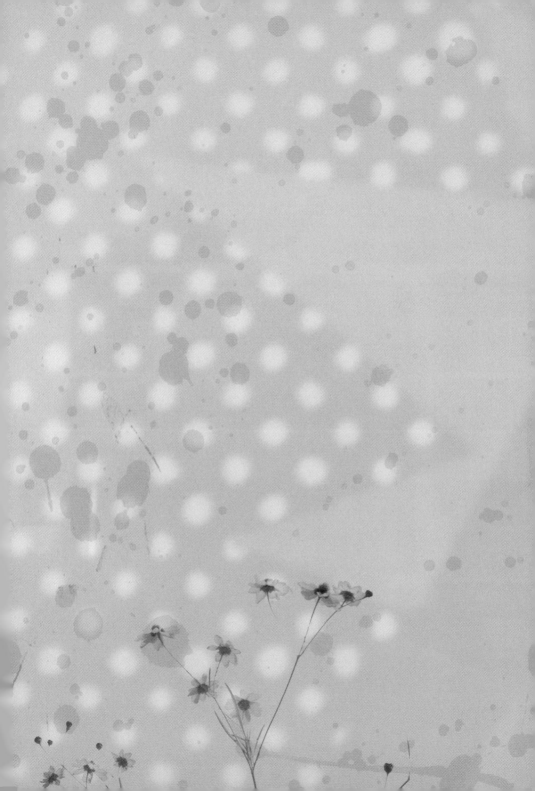

Do you remember the signature tune of *The Golden Girls*? - "Thank you for being my friend". That is what I would like to say, thank to my friends and neighbours in North Great Georges Street, to my family, to my wonderful aunt who lived to 103 and supported me to the very last breath in her body, to the congregation in St. Patrick's Cathedral where I attend every Sunday, to my colleagues and friends in the Oireachtas but most of all to my irreplaceable secretary who takes all the crap from the public and gets none of the public bows. Anyway what I really want to say is a general "thank you all for being my friends".

Senator David Norris

I would like to say thank you to Anne-Marie Casey
by reading her one of the most moving poems I know
about gratitude.
All the best – Joseph O'Connor

When, in disgrace with Fortune and men's eyes,
I all alone beweep my outcast state,
And trouble deaf heaven with my bootless cries,
And look upon myself and curse my fate,
Wishing me like to one more rich in hope,
Featured like him, like him with friends possessed,
Desiring this man's art, and that man's scope,
With what I most enjoy contented least,
Yet in these thoughts myself almost despising,
Haply I think on thee, and then my state,
Like to the lark at break of day arising
From sullen earth, sings hymns at heaven's gate

For thy sweet love remembered such wealth brings,
That then I scorn to change my state with kings

William Shakespeare Sonnet 29

A Song for You – Thank You Kids
'Baby, Don't you worry
'bout a thing
Everything we do is in control.
Baby, Don't worry
'bout a thing
'Cos everything will be just
Like before'

Ferdia Mac Anna

Thank you for all the times you haven't knocked me down as I dashed across the road.

Sophie Gorman

I'm thankful for being in the world for as long as it lasts, and for the friends who continue to make my time here so happy and fun - Quentin Fottrell

Thank you for making me cry with laughter. For making me ache with pride. For endless chatter and impromptu sing-along's. For whispered secrets and salty tears. For sweet kisses. For too-brief hugs, For holding my hand. For sharing the sweets. For reminding me what's important. And for lighting up my life every day.

Niamh Greene

She didn't know me
I wanted her to be happy
I went to your house
I didn't pray, I cried.

Cried for her in her confusion.
Her fears,
For my inability to help her.
I couldn't pray.

She no longer frets
When she sees me,
She smiles.
Thank you Lord.

Mary Rourke

Thank You,
You are the magnet that drew out the best in me. When I was with you
I felt beautiful. When I talked with you I felt smart. You were the mirror
that reflected all that was best in me. Now you are gone but I still walk on
the positive path you left behind.

Alice Taylor

The words "Thank You" can seem like such a small thing to say when something huge happens but its all in the way you say them … like when a lover comes to the surface of a deep satisfied sleep only to whisper "Thank You". No other words sound so sweet.

Love, Brian Kennedy

Thank You
Thinking and thanking differ by one small vowel. I think of all who love me
and I thank them.

Micheal O'Siadhail

If we are each others teachers, every thought of you, however
difficult to admit, is a prayer saying thank you.

Christina Reihill

Thank You – For quiet company on dark roads. Aifric Campbell

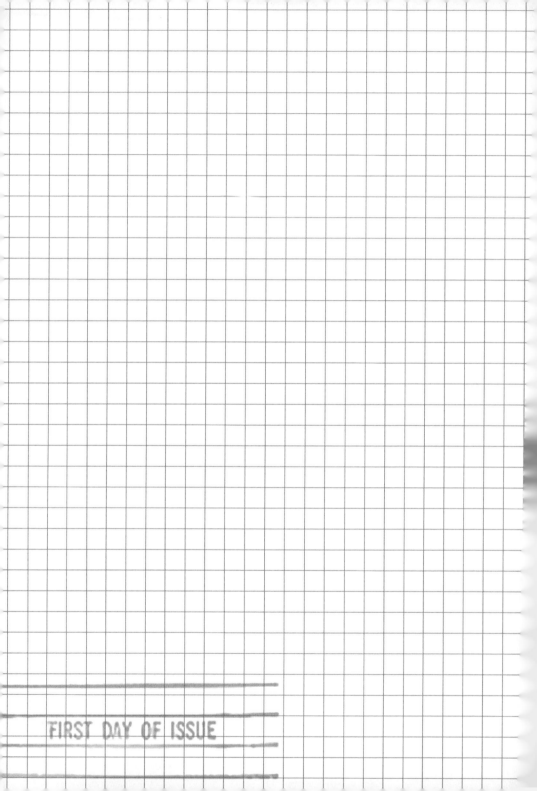

FIRST DAY OF ISSUE

Via Air Mail

RETOUR

INCONNU

If there was a Grown-Ups' Test.
You would be among the Best.
Thanks for the stories that you tell,
And Listening to mine as well.
When I grow up. I tell you true,
I really want to be like you!
Thank You

Gordon Snell

Thank you for that time when I was feeling a bit guilty over you know what and
you said whatever you know what is, what about it.

Eoin Colfer

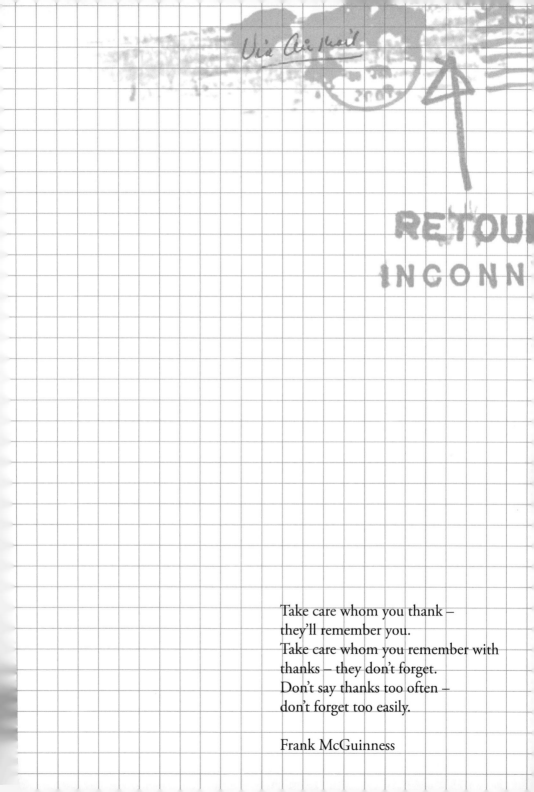

Via Air Mail

RETOU...

INCONN...

Take care whom you thank –
they'll remember you.
Take care whom you remember with
thanks – they don't forget.
Don't say thanks too often –
don't forget too easily.

Frank McGuinness

Thank You

To the nurse from the Mater who rang us. We were at the pictures killing time, awaiting results. We feared the worst; we understood that Christy's cancer had withstood the bucket loads of chemo and radiation he had endured. Last stop was surgery. That call said different.

Rita Ann Higgins

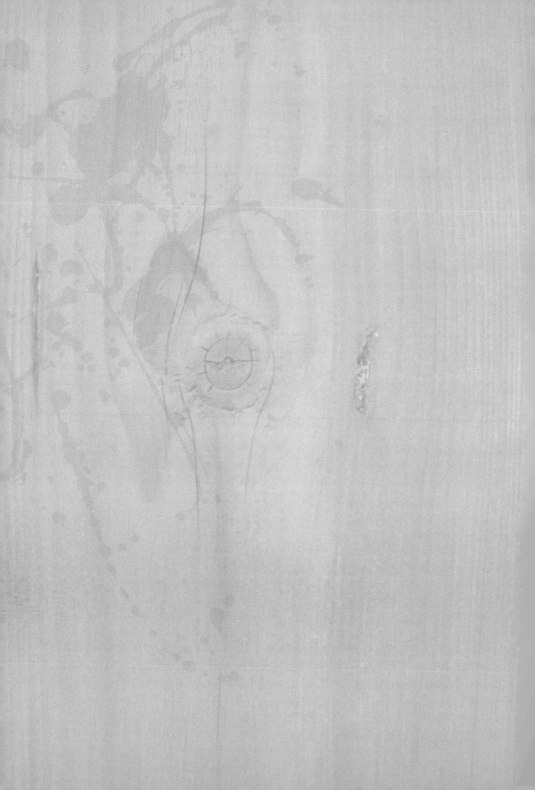

I'm a girl of many words
But for you, just two will do
Thank You, the most important
words of all

Sheila O'Flanagan

Thank you for always instilling in me that I can be whatever
I want to be and giving me the freedom to be creative.

Amanda Grogan

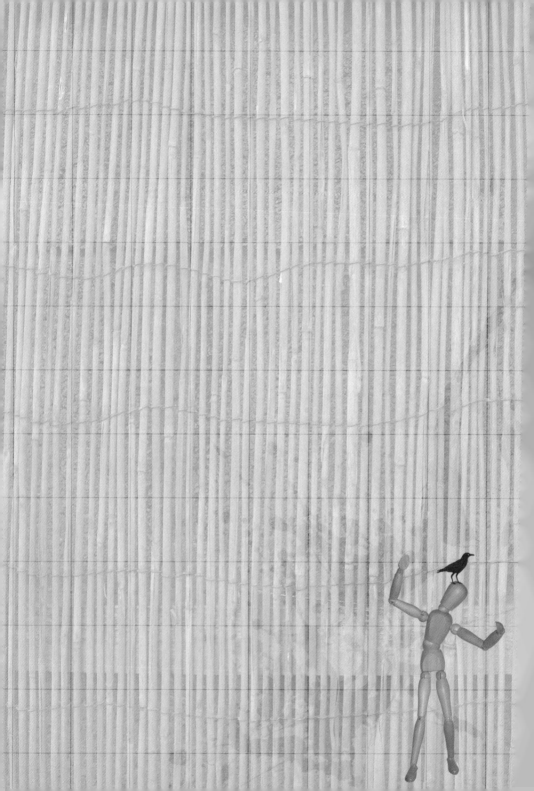

Thank you for listening,
Thank you for understanding,
Thank you for just being you,
But most of all thank you for slagging me
when I became soppy enough to thank you
for listening, understanding and being you.
Don't know what came over me there.

Neil Delamere

Thank you,
For not trying to change me,
For putting up with me,
And for allowing me,
To be me ...

Alan Shortt

Via Air Mail

RETOU
INCONN

THROUGH THE HAPPY TIMES
AND THE SAD,
THE GOOD DAYS
AND THE BAD,
YOU ALWAYS KNEW
HOW TO CARE,
BUT MOST OF ALL
YOU WERE ALWAYS
THERE...

THANK YOU

STEPHEN RAPID

"I am most grateful for your help. Thank you very much"

Brian Friel

To the father of my children – the most special
thank you for those fun unique and wonderful
people – but also for that splendid Italian
portable typewriter that you bought me so many
years ago to replace my father's tacky worn out
one on which I started to write. Thank You.

Jennifer Johnston

Thank you,
For putting the 's'
before every mile
we have travelled together
I will be thankful forever.

Noelle Lynskey

Thank you - for the ability to find out that the real beauty in life is that beauty can actually occur. Go raibh míle maith agaibh go léir.

Colum McCann

I'm a very nervous traveller - always praying for a safe take-off and landing and an end to any turbulence between. One day I was first on board and fell asleep instantly, then jolted awake as we roared down the runway for take-off … no time for any prayer … just this:
"Thank you! It's been wonderful! I couldn't have asked for a better life! Thanks again!"

And that's become my prayer ever since.
Martin Sheen

One day, without knowing it – or maybe you did! – you said the right thing at the right time and turned my life around. All I can say now, never having said it before, is a sincere thank you.

Bernard Farrell

Thank you Maria for your first word – porridge! - Hugo Hamilton

Thank you for holding me
And Saying I could be
Thankyou for Saying "baby"
Thankyou for holding me.

Sinéad O'Connor
XXX

Sinéad O'Connor

Thank You

Thank you for the gift of our children,
for their caring qualities, their lack
of worldliness, their joy in living,
their love, respect and patience,
with us, "Senior Citizens" and with
our "Special Child".

Anna Cronin

Anna Cronin

thanks

thankYou!

STEVESIMPSON·COM

www.fintantaite.com

Thank you...

Niamh Sharkey

Thank you for every new moment... every new day

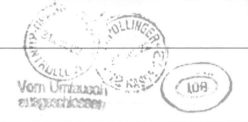

EXPRESSIONS OF THANKS

Below are a selection of the public responses that we received in support of the Thank You Day project.

Thanks! Yesterday was so cool, we should do it more often.
Mary Byrne, Naas

Thank you, for the grace and courage to forgive, and let go.
Gabriel McGovern, Dublin 14

Thank you for seeing the good in me when I lost sight of it myself.
Sinead McAteer, Gweedore

Thank You. You gave me confidence when I had very little.
Katherine Cooke, Fairview

Thank you for never ever saying 'I told you so'.
Johanna Toole, Arklow

Thank you to everyone who has helped us along life's journey and whose efforts we may have taken for granted.
Rita Beattie, Kilkenny

Thank you for that quiet space within me where I know all is well
Teresa O'Dea, Clonakilty

Thank you for loving me, supporting me, praying for me and for being my friend. Heartfelt gratitude each new day.
Anne Soden-Pugh, Rosses Point

Dad, for your understanding, patience and forgiveness, thank you.
Paul Bullman, Youghal

Thank You for being my friends. It means everything to me.
Brendan Macken, Galway

Thank you to all those big beautiful hearts that gave me love, kindness and understanding when I needed it most.
Eileen Kelly, Killiney.

To all those from my past, parents and theirs, all my forebears - I thank you for my life. Without you all, I would not be who I am today. You suffered and did without to give me all I have. Thank you.
Evelyn Corrigan, Monkstown.

Thank you for getting thru' the day an' thank you for helping me get thru', too.
Kevin O'Connor, Ranelagh.

Thank you 'JB' for being the light of my life after 24 years of darkness.
Catherine Hetherington, Drogheda.

Thank you for being there when life cast long gloomy shadows and when joy burst forth in every glorious moment.
Moira O'Sullivan, Kilrush.

Thank you for making me a kid
Neil Kelly, Age 5, Knocklyon.

Thank you to all the children who allowed me to share their lives, hopes and dreams in my teaching career.
Eileen Jordan, Dundalk

I'm thankful for the gift of life. I'm very lucky to have many caring people to look after me forever.
Beth McKeague, Age 11, Dundalk.

Be grateful for adversity, it shows you how strong you are.
Imelda Finn, Blackrock.

Thank you for the intense joy of loving! My darling, my children, my grandchildren, my friends and life.
Anne White, Aughrim.

Thank you for this life and wonderful people who have enriched it.
Julia Lee Dean, Beckenham.

For the unbelievable amount of kindness on the saddest occasion of my life, I say to one and all – my sincerest "Thank You".
Cecily Barry, Dartry.

Thank you, Mam and Dad for bringing me into this world and for loving me the best you could throughout your lives.
Colin Brennan.

Being old (90) and with a walker I am very conscious of how kind people are particularly the young. They open doors and assist me in every way possible. I am most grateful to all of them.
Kathleen Kinsella, Bray.

For your welcoming smile it brought sunshine from behind the clouds on my rainy days. Thank you.
Sadie Barlow, Newbridge.

Thank you for listening and hearing more than words!
Joseph Smith, Skerries.

You broadened my horizons and banished loneliness when you showed me how to use the web. Thank You!
Shaun McCallig, Claremorris.

Thank you Shay for being that very special best friend I wish for everyone.
Paul O'Reilly, Terenure.

Thank you for building me up when I was down and thank you for caring.
Alice O'Regan, Kilmallock.

Thank you for the memories. As the happy and good get stronger and better, the sad and bad fade away.
Regina Brennan, Loughlinstown.

Thank you for the gift of getting to really know my Dad before he died.
Aileen Russell, Tagoat.

Thank you for giving me two beautiful grand-children whose unconditional love, smiles, hugs and kisses lift me up every day.
Angela Hennessy, Clonmel.

Bird Song,
Blue Sky,
Butterfly
Flutters by.
Thank you.
Bríd MacSweeney, Glasnevin.

For all the moments when you smiled hello and the sun and moon shone brighter, thank you.
Gerard Kennedy, Terenure.

Go raibh míle maith agat mo chara – ag eisteacht liom, ag cabhrú liom agus ag gáire chomh maith í gconaí.
Máire Uí Bhroin, Coill Mhic Thomáisín.

Thank you not for what you did for me today, but for doing it with love.
Carmel Kearns, Drimnagh.

Thank you for love and friendships that enrich my life everyday.
Joan Donovan, Galway.

To my cats, for your purrs and miaows, and soft gentle furriness, thank you, thank you.
Ingrid Wallace, Dooradoyle.

Thank you – All the beautiful smiles and listening hearts that light my life with joy.
Theresa Corbett, Cellbridge.

You taught me to stop talking and stay still so I'd find the beauty all round me. Thank you.
Vanda Cummins, Raheny.

Thank you for being my winter solstice, my summer solstice. You watched, you listened, and you cared. You were there – and you told me. I love you. Thank you.
Marie Barrett, Loughrea.

Thank you for the memories that gives every moment deeper colour and meaning.
Máiríde Woods, Sutton.

When you hugged me that day on the street you helped me grow inside. You'll never know how much it meant. Thank you.
Sean O'Reilly, Edmondstown.

I the stranger in the new environment until, your fat affectionate smile enfolded me and drew me in. Thank you.
June Raffery, Enniskerry.

Thank you, thank you, thank you …
Michael Tierney, Sandycove.

Thank you for being the rock upon which I stood.
Dolores Duggan, Kilcolgan.

Thank you so much for being so kind. You helped me cross the road.
Mary Walsh, Hollymount.

Thank you for years of faithfulness, companionship and joy (now tears!) from our beautiful black dog, Rago.
Connie Reid, Enniskerry.

Thank you for yesterday. It journeyed me to today, and today I see the wisdom of yesterday. My soul dances in the light.
Cathy Bell-Howlett, Waterford.

Míle buíochas for: gach lá, gach rud, gach duine i mo shaol. Go raibh maith agat.
Bróna Uí Loing, Rathchúil.

We cannot be thankful for every situation but we can find something to be thankful for in every situation.
Pauline Hughes, Gorey.

Please and thank you are free, but the returns are rich.
Nike Ruf, Baldoyle.

Thanking costs nothing and the thanking is free but the recognition of gratitude is priceless indeed. Thank you for this opportunity to have said so. Cheers!
Sonja Bunker, Athlone.

Thank you God, for the gift of creativity.
Sarah Butler.

Thank you shows appreciation for a gift, a word, a thought. A little phrase from childhood that we have all been taught.
Suzanne Hayes, Glenageary.

According to Chinese wisdom we should express profound daily gratitude for life's five greatest blessings – happiness, health, wholeness, peace, longevity.
Dr Mary H. O'Sullivan, Cork.

Thank a million guardian angel. No appointments necessary with you. Call and talk anytime, secrets, tell you all. Thanks again.
Eileen Fitzpatrick, Wexford.

Thank you creator spirit, for the healing powers of the sea – a soothing balm for weary body, mind and soul.
Fiona Murdoch, Dublin 16.

Thank you for each new day, each day is a new beginning, a rebirth, another chance to be more loving.
Aoife Nelson, Dublin 6.

Thank you God for letting me live.
Barry O'Sullivan, Glasnevin Age 6.

Thank you for showing the gift of your laughter when I thought I could never smile again.
Ger Gallagher, Cabinteely.

Thank you for the sound of my children's laughter.
Yvonne McBride, Carlingford

For the high road above
Lake Sliabh na gCeart
where the cuckoo sings.
My walk on the moon.
Jean Tuomey, Castlebar.

For being in a happy place today
After our nightmare year
Your unexpected support
Meant everything to us
Thank You
Carmel Ryan, Donaghmede.

Thank you to my Dad. He gave the drink up on a whim, and I thought he was mad. After one year off it, he said it was the greatest year of his life. Now I'm 6 months off it and ditto!
Peter Fitzsimons

A knowledge that living each moment is as good as it gets – I am thankful for being alive, being present.
Anne Hennessy, Dublin 18.

Enjoying life through the senses
Thankful for each moment life brings
Taste, smell, sight, hearing
Flavours, roses, colours – bible songs
Anne Hennessy, Dublin 18.

I am grateful for;
• love of family and friends,
• an education that highlighted the importance of values.
• the joy gained from nature, (walking alone but not feeling alone),
• an awareness of the role emotions play in my life and in relationships,
• the ability to see the funny side of life and to enjoy and treasure times of feeling 'this is perfect',

• having had loving parents.
… and so much more!
Shelagh McGrogan, Belfast.

Thank you to organ donors and their families. Their generosity has given others so much to be grateful for.
Geraldine Breslin, Bundoran.

Thank you for thanking me….
Mary Brennan, Monasterboice.

Thank you for all that is you and the abundance of you.
Pauline McLoughlin, Sligo.

Everyday I am so thankful for my wonderful husband and the lovely kicks I get in my tummy from our unborn baby.
Joanne Ormond, Dundrum.

Thank you for learning to smile, it's making the night feeds a lot easier.
Julie Heffernan, Terenure.

Thank you to my family and friends for walking with me on my journey with cancer. Forever grateful. Love and hope.
Cathy McCarthy, Stillorgan.

Thank you for putting your hand on my shoulder in radiotherapy and saying my treatment was going great.
Francis Foran, Firhouse.

Your thoughtfulness shows in everything you do, thank you.
Jim Devoy, Portmarnock.

Thank you for reminding me that good health is worth more than all the world's wealth.
Geraldine Birch, Belfast.

Thank you for teaching me how to change the mundane school runs into cherished moments.
Una Griffin, Ranelagh.

Thank you for 'hanging out' with Granny.
Norma Treacy, Dublin 15.

It costs nothing, it means so much, so why not
say it. Thank you.
Lorraine Callan, Coolock.

Thank you for providing such caring nursing
staff to my sister-in-law during her final days in
October 2009.
Winifred Hogan, Artane.

Thank you for stopping to tell me how brave I
was to make a major change in my life.
Catherine Bland, Greystones.

My mantra in life is better to be born lucky
than rich and everyday is living proof for me.
So thank you.
Anna Malone, Rathfarnham.

Thank you for reminding me to say thank you.
For that I am very grateful.
Avril Murphy Allen, Killiney.

You're precious and dear,
When I fret with unnecessary fear,
You cajole me into good cheer.
Go raibh maith agat.
Bridie McAndrew, Ballina.

Than you for the enduring blessings that your
love brings to illuminate my life.
Love never ends.
Mary F. McAteer, Kilmeague.

Thank you for the gift of friends and friendships.
Patricia Boate, Greystones.

Thanks to the sunshine, for opening the blossoms.
Thanks to the cuckoo for reminding us of summer
even if you 'lay out'.
Anne Taylor, Claremorris.

Busy bees pluck nectar from flowers in evening
sunshine.
Life giving.
Mary Casey, Claremorris.

WHEN MY HEAD CHURNS AND SPINS
AT 3 OR 4 AM
WITH ISSUES OF THE DAY, I FEEL
YOUR ARMS COME ROUND ME.
YOUR SLEEPING BODY CLOSE TO MINE,
YOUR STEADY BREATHING
FEELING SAFE.

THIS IS WHAT MATTERS.
THIS IS ENOUGH.
THIS IS MORE THAN ENOUGH.

Helen Collins

I wish that my words could express
The thanks that wells up in my breast,
You have blessed me.
Angela MacNamara, Dublin 14

Thank you for the reflection of our love that I
see in the face of our "three" beautiful children.
Thank you.
Ann Hughes, Sligo.

Thank you should be heard regularly by children
at home.
Imelda C. Keogh, Killiney.

It's easy to say 'thank you' almost every day and
surprising to find everyone too will copy what
you say!
Sylvia Vincent, Raheny.

A day that I fail to say thank you to someone or
for something is for me a wasted day.
Sean Donegan, Salthill.

The day my Man died a glance at her calendar
said "One kind word can light up three winter
months."
Áine Whelan, Glasnevin.

Thank you for the soft day, wind from the west, light on the water.
Grace Neville, Cork.

I thank God for my five wonderful children and two grand children, for their health, and the love they give.
Jennifer Masterson, Baldoyle.

Thanks to my Dad who instilled in my psyche two phrases – count your blessings and stickability.
Claire Walsh, Cork.

Thank you - breath.
With every breath I breathe you fill me with new life. Renewing and bringing hope in every way, to every living being.
Louisa Schewe, Crosshaven.

Thank you for the gratitude created for all through integrating those with disabilities into the fabric of our daily lives.
Ciaran McGettrick, Glenageary.

It's great to be alive. Thank you God.
Elizabeth Shekleton, Blackrock.

At the end of the day in God's presence, I gather up all the goodness and the light in gratitude.
Mary Coyle, Drogheda.

The forty foot and all its amazing swimmers. No medication works better. Impossible to leave but on a high, thank you.
Jean Greene, Killiney.

Thank you for the kindness
and generosity of strangers;
the gifts of music
colour, flowers, birds and
animals that we see daily.
John McGurk, Tourmakeady.

Dear C.
Thank you for listening while I sobbed for Ireland (on the life and death of my baby granddaughter).
Catriona Brennan, Shanakiel.

To see beyond the trivia and the sadness of life, to what is real. For that, I am truly thankful.
Yvonne Townson, Killiney.

I will forever be grateful for the never ending efforts given towards my autistic son Aiden by his teachers.
May Treanor, Delvin.

Thank you to the wonderful staff in Kiltipper Woods Care Centre who are looking after both of my parents – reblessed assurance.
Stephanie Sadlier, Knocklyon.

Thank you to the two ladies who gave me, by adoption, two treasures, Emma (26) and Cormac (22).
Happy Mum – Margaret Ryan, Navan.

Thanks Dave for all your love. It's still around us though you're above.
Dave Morris, 28th July 2009, Aged 53 yrs.
Valerie O'Reilly, Terenure.

Thank you to my family for arranging the most amazing "surprise" party to celebrate my 80th Birthday.
Mrs. Pat Fitzgibbon, Gort.

To everyone who ensures that people can *live* up to the last second in dignity, joy, music, dancing, hugs, kisses and friendship!
Adrienne Donnelly, Foxrock.

Thank you for the blessings of my loving parents who made it to their 50th wedding anniversary this year still holding hands.
Máire Ní Dhomhnaill, Báile Na hAbhainn.

For the growing awareness of the abundance of love, wonder and celebration along this journey – thank you.
Moira Byrne, Rahoon.

Dear Lord, Thank you for bringing me to this day. Please give me the grace to live it well.
Margaret Ferguson, Parteen.

St Francis Hospice, Raheny.
Thank you for giving me permission to be my dad's daughter rather than his doctor.
Adrienne Foran, Clontarf.

When you were at you lowest ebb, you thought of and gave to others. Thank you.
Elizabeth Eager, Kilcoole.

My final prayer at the close of the day "Thank you Lord for all you have given, and all you have taken away."
Nóra Prendergast, Churchtown.

An Attitude of Gratitude!
Precious thank-yous to all our midwives and childcare minders – truly angels on earth.
Fionnuala Darby, Waterville. Dublin 15.

Dear God
Thank you for my husband, my family, my friends, my garden, cats, dogs, swimming, cycling, singing and you.
Sheila Murphy, Monaghan.

Thank you thought for the day!
When a giver becomes the receiver of "Thank you", the cycle is complete.
Norma Sexton, Blackrock.

Thank you to my three wonderful children – Rory, Séamus and Luan because you have filled my life with joy!
Clare Beirne, Dun Laoire.

Thank you for the pets, past and present in our household – Hamish, Billy, Heather, Holly, MacDuff, Pud, Miranda and Sweetie Pie.
Anne O'Curry, Foxrock.

Maith thú
Thank you
Siobhán Ní Chuanáigh, Ranallach.

My Mum told me she saw the programme on Alzheimer's. "What was it about" I asked, "I forget" she replied! Thank you Mum. We laughed together. My Mum has Alzheimer's.
Sheelagh Jones, Enniskerry.

Thank you for our beautiful daughter Amanda.
Born 10/9/1974
Died 24/4/1977
Aged 2 and a 1/2.
Maura and John Rosers, Greystones.

I thank the lord that I have survived pancreatic cancer.
I say 'thank you' for my wonderful family.
I thank God for my friends.
I thank God for my neighbours.
I thank God for the beauty of nature and this country.
Eithne Murphy, Dundrum.

Thank you to everyone who came to us and helped us during our little daughter's short life, it gave us great comfort to feel that support and love.
Feb '96 – Nov '96.
Geraldine Burke, Naas.

Thanks for sparing Mam and Dad to see me grow up, thanks for sparing me to bring my children up. Thanks for my grandchildren.
Rose Dowling, Dublin 22.

Thank you for playing that well loved hymn so beautifully during Holy Communion to make it truly a holy moment.
Cherry Watkins, Maynooth.

Thank you to the hospice for helping my mother die in comfort and with peace and dignity.
Patricia Carey, Blackrock.

Thank ye for giving me the good genes and the odd ones – I wouldn't be without them.
Donal A. Murphy, Nenagh.

For 'scorning not his simplicity' as you cradled me in your arms and wiped away my tears, thank you.
Ita Condon, Raheen.

My husband has Huntington's disease; my two children have a 50% chance of inheriting the disease. Still I am thankful that all of this has made me a better person.
Bernadette Spellman, Fairview.

Nature lays a mantel over countryside for everyone to enjoy, pondering the wonderment and joy of its creation. Míle Buíochas.
Bríd Dean-McAndrews, Ballina.

Thank you for my health.
Thank you for my family.
Mary Casey, Claremorris.

Thank you Lord Jesus for dying on the cross for me and all mankind.
Avril Deacon, Bunclody.

Thank you for me.
Martina McGann, Clonee.

Thank you God for my fishing rod,
Casting for trout,
Stillness throughout,
A gentle nod,
Thank you God.
Ger Dowling, Ballintemple.

Thank you Mam for encouraging me always to say those two simple words of 'thank you' …it channels healthy energy.
Mary Regan, Tallaght.

I am grateful for the abundance and love that is brought to me daily by my family and my God.
Lynne Barker, Lusk.

Thank you for choosing to live.
Úna Flanagan, Ballyhaunis.

Thank you for helping me to accept the things I cannot change.
Noreen Edwards.

To an ex – Thank you for leaving me, I turned my life around, it was the best gift you could have given me, thank you.
Sandra Harris, Dublin 2.

Thank you for: the blood in my veins, the air in my lungs, the thoughts in my head and the love in my heart.
D. Kernaghan, Belfast.

Thank you kindly.
Ann Cannon, Tallaght.

Pupils of Dún Dealgan N.S, Dundalk

Thank you for my family.
Daniel Carr, Age 11

Thank you friends and family.
Jordan Smartt

I am thankful we have good food and clean water in Ireland.
Sarah Burns, Age 12

Thank you for food and drink.
Adam Shields, Age 12

I am thankful for my family and the people around me.
Rachel Rice, Age 11

I'm thankful for my life and everyone in it.
Damilda Fagbamila.

Thank you for my family being alive and well.
Aoibhinn Fleming.

Thank you very very much.
Andrew Duffy

ACKNOWLEDGEMENTS

Thank You Day Project Concept
Bill Hughes

Thank You Book Concept
Niamh O'Carroll

Project Team
Róisín Ingle
Eileen Pearson
Stephen Averill
Eugene Murray
Tim O'Dea
Angela Kerr
Kirana Bhagwan

Special Thanks

All the contributors who provided
the inspiration for the book
Dr Marie Murray
Sinead O'Connor
Gisele Scanlon, Bren B, James Cooper, Steve Simpson,
P.J. Lynch, Niamh Sharkey, Fintan Tait and Doreen Kennedy
Ita Gibney, Marika MacCarvill and Phil Boughton of Gibney Communications
John Lynch, Number 10 Ormond Quay
Kevin Barry
Laura Rooney Ferris
Mary Wilson and Marian Richardson at Drivetime.
The Irish Times
Windmill Lane Recording Studios
Windmill Lane Creative Post Production
Emer Connolly
Mags Walsh and Children's Books Ireland
Eilish Wren and Listowel Writers Week,
Amber Kehoe and the Flat Lakes Festival
Sara O'Donovan and the West Cork Literary Festival